Take Me Along

THE BEST ^Substitute TEACHER'S SURVIVAL GUIDE YET!

by Lynn Videon, Cathy McDuffie, Judith Stopper

Fearon Teacher Aids
A Division of Frank Schaffer Publications, Inc.

This Fearon Teacher Aids product was formerly manufactured and distributed by American Teaching Aids, Inc., a subsidiary of Silver Burdett Ginn, and is now manufactured and distributed by Frank Schaffer Publications, Inc. FEARON, FEARON TEACHER AIDS, and the FEARON balloon logo are marks used under license from Simon & Schuster, Inc.

Illustrator: Barry Geller

ISBN 0-8224-6719-4

Printed in the United States of America

1. 9

CONTENTS

PREFACE

Every day is your first day of teaching when you are a substitute teacher! You're guaranteed to experience unfamiliar curricula, different grade levels, different students, and new building locations. And you can always expect the unexpected.

What happens when the twenty-minute lesson plan ends in five minutes, the slide projector won't work, the classroom worksheets are missing, the art teacher is absent, the teacher's manual is not there, or the extension cords are gone? When a substitute teacher is taking the place of the regular teacher, the classroom routine won't be the same.

Next time, instead of being frustrated by unexpected situations, take advantage of the opportunity to change the routine and supplement the lesson plans with interesting and creative activities from this book.

Take Me Along was written by substitute teachers *who have been there!* We have combined up-to-date learning activities and longtime favorites to make this handbook. This resource is a *must* for teachers who want:

- an organized, easy-to-use format
- learning activities that do not require extensive materials
- simplified instructions
- flexible instructional levels

So when the telephone rings to notify you of your next substitute job, accept with confidence knowing that this handbook will help you get through the day.

SURVIVAL TIPS FOR SUBSTITUTE TEACHERS

Organize Yourself

- Find the location of essential rooms other than your assigned classroom: main office, lavatories, nurse's office, library, gymnasium, multipurpose room, and cafeteria.

- Take along a book or magazine that has stories that are suitable to read to primary and intermediate students.

- Dress in versatile clothing in case you have extra duties such as outdoor recess or bus dismissal.

- Take a "break" bag that could include coffee, tea, a snack, and a cup. Include headache tablets if new situations make you tense.

- Be sure that you have this book, *Take Me Along*, to supplement the classroom teacher's lesson plans with well-planned, interesting games and activities.

Use Classroom Management Techniques

- BE AT SCHOOL EARLY to acquaint yourself with classroom procedures, lesson plans, and students.

- BE READY TO BEGIN an activity as soon as students arrive.

- BE AWARE of students' signs of restlessness, frustration, or boredom. Be willing to change activities and plans when students have reached their saturation points.

- BE FLEXIBLE in following the classroom teacher's lesson plans. Some teachers write extensive plans to make sure there's plenty to do. If a forty-minute plan is lasting longer than appropriate, end the lesson and leave an explanatory note for the teacher.

- BE FIRM in following the established rules of the classroom. Let students know which behavior patterns you find acceptable and which ones are unacceptable. Remember that disciplinary techniques differ for primary and intermediate students.

- BE CONSISTENT in disciplining students so they will learn what type of behavior you expect.
- BE IN CONTROL and maintain control. Try the following techniques:

  Wait for student attention and inform the students that you are waiting.

  Vary the tone and volume of your voice, but remember that quiet, firm tones achieve more than shouting.

  Use gestures, such as fingers to the lips, to give messages.

  Separate students who seem to encourage their neighbors to create disturbances.

  Discipline only the students who demonstrate inappropriate behavior. Undeserved blanket punishments generate animosity.

  Follow through on discipline that you have threatened.

  Ignore minor misbehavior if you think it is only an attention-getting device.

  Take action when a student's behavior may be injurious to that student or to others. Don't hesitate to enlist the help of another teacher or the principal if you need assistance in halting a disturbance.

  Reinforce and reward good behavior.

GETTING ACQUAINTED

Most people respond favorably when they are called by name. Though it may be difficult to learn each student's name in the short time that you may be with a class, it is worth the effort. The students will appreciate your interest, and you'll feel more organized.

Here are some quick and easy activities to help you get acquainted with the students. There are two types of activities in this section: introductions and making nameplates.

The activities for introductions will help you learn the students' names as you learn something about each individual. They require little or no preparation and can be completed within a few minutes.

The nameplate activities are helpful as opening activities. They require few materials and only brief explanations. The students can be making their nameplates while you are getting organized for the day. Plus, the nameplates make attractive cue cards as you face the class.

INTRODUCTIONS

Bumpity-Bump

Materials
none

Procedure
- Direct students to stand in a circle.
- Select a student to be the first caller. The student caller stands in the center of the circle.
- The caller names a student on the circle and then says the word *right* or *left* immediately after the student's name.
- The student who was named must then name the person on the right or left before the caller says "Bumpity-bump!"
- Failure to accomplish this sends the student named by the caller into the center, and the caller escapes.

Hello, I'm . . .

Materials
none

Procedure
- Have the students sit in a circle.
- Begin the activity by saying, "I'm (your name) and I like to (one of your hobbies). This is (name of a student)."
- The student you name must then introduce himself, or herself, name a hobby, and repeat your introduction. This student must also name the next student on the circle. For example: "My name is Pat, and I like to swim. This is (teacher's name), and she likes to hike. This is Kelly."
- Each student in turn tries to name all the persons previously introduced and repeat what each one likes.

Cue Card Introductions

Materials

3″ × 5″ index cards (or small pieces of paper)

pencil, chalkboard, chalk

Procedure

- Write the following list on the chalkboard:

    name
    hair color
    favorite television show
    favorite dessert
    favorite game

- Pass an index card to each student.

- Direct the students to complete their cards with the information outlined on the chalkboard.

- Collect and shuffle the cards. Select a card and introduce the student to the class.

- The student who was just introduced then selects a card and makes a similar introduction. The activity continues until everyone has been introduced.

Variation

To play a guessing game, select a card and read all the information except the student's name. Have the students in the class guess who is being described.

MAKING NAMEPLATES

Basic Nameplates

Materials
8½″ × 11″ manila or white drawing paper

pencil, crayons or markers

Procedure
Distribute the paper and have the students:

- Fold their papers into thirds.

- Print their names clearly on the outside of the middle third of their papers.

- Decorate the nameplates with crayons or markers.

- Stand the nameplates on their desks so that the names are visible to anyone in the front of the classroom.

Name Designs

Materials
8½″ × 11″ manila or construction paper

pencil, crayons or markers

Procedure
- Demonstrate several ways to write or print letters of the alphabet.

- Distribute the paper and direct the students to fold their papers into thirds.

- Give students five to ten minutes to design their names in the middle third of the paper. (Suggest to the students that they might want to practice their designs on scrap paper before they work on the final nameplate.)

- Have students stand the nameplates on their desks.

Executive Nameplates

Materials

4½″ × 11″ manila or
construction paper

markers or crayons, pencil

Procedure

- Briefly discuss the meaning of the word *executive*. For example, "What is an executive?", "Who is an executive in our school?"

- Tell the class that they are soon to be executives with nameplates on their desks.

- Distribute the paper, then direct the students to fold their papers into thirds.

- Allow five to ten minutes for the students to design their nameplates. When completed, the nameplates should stand on the desks with the students' names facing the front of the classroom.

Picture Me

Materials

8½″ × 11″ manila or
construction paper

crayons or markers, pencil

Procedure

- Tell the class a bit about yourself—your interests, hobbies.

- Elicit examples of the students' hobbies and interests and list some of them on the chalkboard.

- Distribute the paper and direct the students to fold their sheets into thirds.

- Using the space in the middle third of the papers, the students print their names and draw pictures that show their interests or hobbies.

- Direct the students to stand the nameplates on their desks, with the names facing the front of the classroom.

Describe Yourself

Materials
8½″ × 11″ manila or construction paper

crayons or markers, pencil, chalkboard, chalk

Procedure
- Discuss the use of adjectives.

- Brainstorm several adjectives and write them on the chalkboard.

- Draw a sample nameplate on the chalkboard. Choose adjectives that begin with each letter of the sample name (see example).

- Distribute the paper. Have the students fold their papers into thirds and print their names vertically on the outside of the middle third of the folded papers (see example).

- Direct the students to write adjectives that begin with the letters of their names.

- Have students stand the nameplates on their desks.

ART

The activities in this section use only materials that are standard art supplies or household items. The project descriptions are divided into two groups, nonseasonal and seasonal. In the non-seasonal group, simpler activities are presented first and the more complex activities follow. In the seasonal group, activities are organized in sequence according to the school year: fall, winter, spring. This will help you in planning which activities to use with a particular group. Since all the activities are uncomplicated, you can modify them to suit your needs.

With younger students, present directions step-by-step. It is sometimes useful to show the steps on the chalkboard.

There are three activities that use teacher-prepared patterns. These are: Fire Truck, Shamrock Rubbings, and Lucky Potato Person. The patterns are very simple to make, but it's helpful to have prepared them in advance.

NONSEASONAL ART ACTIVITIES

Abstract Scribble Designs

Materials
8½″ × 11″ manila paper

crayons

Procedure
Have each student:

- Use a black crayon to draw curved lines over the paper without lifting the crayon. The lines should cross at several points to form a scribble with many open spaces.

- Color each open space with a different color.

  Note: You might demonstrate the scribble so students can see how to leave spaces large enough to color. Younger students would benefit from practice with a piece of scrap paper.

Paper Mosaics

Materials
paper—8½″ × 11″ manila or white construction paper, scraps or small pieces of construction paper of several colors

pencil, scissors, glue

Procedure
Have each student:

- Draw a simple object on the manila or white paper. (Older students might draw a detailed object or scene.)

- Cut out small squares of paper from different colors of the construction paper scraps.

- Glue the squares into the drawing, filling in the object or objects.

Animal Mosaics

Materials
paper—8½″ × 11″ manila,
8½″ × 11″ dark color
construction paper,
scraps or small pieces of
construction paper of
several colors

pencil, scissors, glue

Procedure
Have each student:

- Draw a large animal on the manila paper and cut it out.

- Cut several small pieces of colored construction paper from scraps into simple shapes of various sizes.

- Glue the cutout shapes on the animal, overlapping them. (This will make the mosaic.)

- Glue the completed animal mosaic on the dark color construction paper.

Fire Truck

Materials
six to eight fire truck
patterns sized to fit
4½″ × 11″ paper

construction paper—
4½″ × 11″ red, 4½″ × 11″ black

pencil, scissors, glue, crayons

Procedure
Have each student:

- Trace a truck pattern on the red paper. Pass the pattern to a neighbor.

- Cut out the truck form.

- Make a ladder by cutting two long strips and many short strips from the black paper.

- Cut wheels from the black paper.

- Glue all the parts together to make a fire truck.

- Use crayons to add the finishing touches.

Animals in Circus Cages

Materials
construction paper—
8½″ × 11″ white, 8½″ × 11″ black, 8½″ × 11″ blue

pencil, ruler, crayons or markers, scissors, glue

Procedure
Have each student:

- Draw a large animal on the white construction paper. Color the animal and cut it out.

- Glue the animal on the blue construction paper.

- Cut long strips of black paper. Cut the paper strips horizontally or vertically to match the height (top to bottom) of the blue paper.

- Glue the strips on the blue paper and on top of the animal to form a cage.

- Cut two circles from the black paper and glue them at the bottom of the cage to form wheels.

Crayon Etchings

Materials
5½″ × 8½″ manila paper

crayons, paper towel or facial tissue, toothpick

Procedure
Have each student:

- Color the manila paper completely with several bright colors. (Pressure on the crayon should be heavy so that a solid layer of wax is left on the paper.)

- Wipe the paper lightly with a facial tissue or paper towel to remove the small flakes of wax.

- Color over all the colors with black crayon, again applying pressure to achieve a heavy coat of wax.

- Etch a picture using the toothpick to scratch away black crayon and expose lines of color from beneath. The etching can be a simple design or an elaborate picture.

Greeting Cards

Materials
construction paper—
8½″ × 11″ white or other light color student writing paper

pencil, crayons

Procedure
Have each student:

- Choose an appropriate greeting: Happy Holidays, Get Well, Happy Birthday, Congratulations, and so on.

- Write the greeting vertically in uppercase letters on a sheet of student writing paper.

- Use each letter to begin a word that is appropriate to the occasion.

- Fold the construction paper in half to form a card.

- Copy the greeting from the writing paper onto the front of the card.

- Decorate the card with crayons and write a message inside.

Positive and Negative Designs

Materials

construction paper—
8½″ × 11″ black, 8½″ × 11″
in nine colors (three
shades of each primary
color)

pencil, scissors, glue

Procedure

Distribute four sheets of construction paper to each student—one black and three shades of one primary color. Have each student:

- Make a simple drawing of an object (a piece of fruit, tree, leaf, and so on) on one of the sheets of primary color construction paper.

- Cut out the drawing. Trace it on the papers that are in the other two shades of the same color. Cut out these two drawings.

- Overlap the three drawings or arrange them in a design on the black construction paper. The drawings may be cut in halves or thirds if desired.

- Once a design is arranged, glue it into place.

One-Shape Art

Materials
drawing paper

pencil, crayons

Procedure
Have each student:

- Decide on a shape to use in the drawing, for example, a triangle, a circle, or a square.

- Draw a picture of an animal or object, using various sizes of only one shape.

- Color the drawing.

SEASONAL ART ACTIVITIES

Leaf Rubbings

Materials
one leaf for each student

manila or white drawing paper

crayons

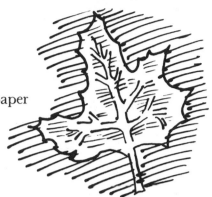

Procedure
Have each student:

- Select a leaf.
- Place the leaf under the manila or white drawing paper.
- Hold the paper tightly so the leaf will not slide.
- Use a crayon to color back and forth over the leaf until the outline of the entire leaf appears.
- Move the leaf to a new position under the paper and repeat the coloring with another crayon.
- Make three to five rubbings.

  Note: It may be possible to take the class on a short walk to collect leaves. However, before you plan a walk, be sure to check with the principal—school policies differ.

Torn-Paper Trees

Materials
construction paper—
8½″ × 11″ blue, 4¼″ × 11″
brown, scraps or small
pieces of several fall
colors

scissors, glue

Procedure
Have each student:

- Cut a tree trunk from the brown paper.

- Glue the trunk on the blue background.

- Tear small shapes for leaves from the fall-color construction paper.

- Glue the pieces on the trunk to form a brightly colored tree top. (Some pieces may be added to represent fallen leaves.)

- Add finishing touches (sky, grass, sun, and so on).

Halloween Cat

Materials
construction paper—
8½″ × 11″ black, scraps or
small pieces of several
colors

scissors, glue

Procedure
Have each student:

- Fold the piece of black paper in half with the longer sides together.

- Cut out a semicircle from the center of the side that is opposite the fold.

- Use one semicircle for the head. Glue the curved side on the body.

- Cut a tail from the other semicircle. Glue it inside the end that is opposite to the head.

- Cut two triangle-ears, a nose, mouth, and whiskers from the scraps of construction paper.

- Glue the features on the cat.

Halloween Chalk Drawings

Materials
construction paper—
8½″ × 11″ black or navy blue

bright colored chalks

Procedure
Have each student use bright colored chalks on the dark paper to draw one of the following pictures.

- a night scene with the moon, children out for trick-or-treat, lights shining in a house

- a picture showing what a witch might have in the kitchen, how she might travel, or where she might live

- some scary ghosts, a haunted house, a bright moon

- a self-portrait in costume

Ghostly Portraits

Materials
construction paper—
8½″ × 11″ white,
8½″ × 11″ black, scraps or
small pieces of several
colors

pencil, scissors, glue

Procedure
Have each student:

- Draw a large ghost on the white construction paper.

- Cut out the ghost and glue it on the black construction paper.

- Cut out facial features from the construction paper scraps. Glue them to the ghost.

- Add other interesting details such as hats, neckties, ribbons, necklaces, and buttons.

Pumpkin Head

Materials
construction paper—
8½″ × 11″ orange, 8½″ × 11″
yellow

pencil, scissors, glue

Procedure
Have each student:

- Cut the four corners off the orange paper, rounding the rectangle to form a head.

- Draw large facial features on the orange head.

- Cut out the facial features.

- Glue the orange head on the yellow paper.

Halloween Witch

Materials

construction paper—
4¼″ × 11″ black, 8½″ × 11″
white

pencil, scissors, glue,
crayons

Procedure

Have each student:

- Cut a tall triangle from the black paper. Glue it on the white construction paper. It will be the witch's dress.

- Draw and color a head on the top of the triangle-dress.

- Cut a small triangle from the black paper to be the witch's hat. Glue it on the head.

- Cut strips of black paper for the witch's arms and broomstick.

- Use crayons to add broom bristles, hair, feet, and other details.

Tissue-and-Paper Ghosts

Materials
construction paper—
5½″ × 8½″ black or orange,
4¼″ × 5½″ white, 8″ × 8″
tissue paper or standard
size facial tissue

scissors, glue, crayons

Procedure
Have each student:

- Cut out a circle from the white construction paper. Glue only the top half of the circle onto the orange or black paper.

- Glue one white facial tissue or a small piece of tissue paper under the unglued portion of the circle.

- Draw a face.

- Add decorations to the background.

Five-Fingered Turkey

Materials
manila paper
crayons

Procedure
Have each student:

- Spread one hand in the center of the paper. Trace around it with a brown crayon.

- Color the thumb as the turkey's head and the fingers as the feathers.

- Color the rest of the body. Add a wing, legs, beak, and wattle.

- Draw and color scenery around the turkey.

Turkey Greeting

Materials

construction paper—
8½″ × 11″ white, 5½″ × 8½″
brown, 1″ × 5½″ strips of
several colors, scraps or
small pieces of several
colors

pencil, scissors, glue,
crayons

Procedure

Have each student:

- Fold the white paper in half so that the shorter edges are together.

- Cut off the corners to give the card rounded edges.

- Place the card on the desk or table so that it is face up.

- Cut a large and a small circle out of the brown paper.

- Cut out six feathers from the strips of colored paper.

- Arrange the brown circles and feathers to form a turkey (head, body, and feathers).

- Glue the feathers to the card first. Then glue the body (larger circle) on top of the feathers. Last, glue the head (smaller circle) on the body. (See illustration.)

- Use scraps of paper to make facial features. Glue them to the head.

- Write a Thanksgiving message inside the card.

Menorah

Materials
construction paper—
8½″ × 11″ white, 8½″ × 5½″
yellow, 4¼″ × 5½″ red

pencils, scissors, glue,
crayons

Procedure
Have each student:

- Draw the body of a menorah on the white paper with a black crayon.

- Cut seven yellow strips for candles. Glue each strip to the crayon form of the menorah.

- Cut seven red flames for the top of each candle. Glue them in place.

Holiday-Links Garland

Materials
construction paper—8½″ × 11″ green and red

scissors, pencil, ruler, glue

Procedure
Have each student:

- Use a ruler and pencil to draw straight lines along the shorter width of both the red and green sheets of paper. (Demonstrate this for younger students.)

- Cut along each penciled line to make several strips of red and green paper.

- Form one strip into a loop. Glue the ends together to hold the loop.

- Form and glue more loops, each one through the previous loop. Alternate red and green.

Reindeer

Materials
construction paper—
8½″ × 11″ brown, 8½″ × 11″
yellow

ruler, pencil, scissors, glue

Procedure
Have each student:

- Measure along the longer edge of the paper and make a mark at five-and-one-half inches.

- Use the ruler to draw a straight line from the pencil mark to both corners on the opposite edge of the paper.

- Cut on the lines to each corner, creating a triangle-face.

- Turn the paper so that the eleven-inch edge is the top edge. Use the scissors to cut off the bottom point and form a rounded snout.

- Trace each hand on the yellow paper. Cut out the hands.

- Glue the hands behind the triangle-head to make antlers.

- Use scraps of yellow to make the eyes and the tip of the nose. Glue these features on the triangle-face.

Holiday Drawings

Materials
manila paper

crayons

Procedure
Have the students:

- Fold the paper into four parts.

- Draw and color a picture in each part. Here are some suggested pictures:

> students and their families eating a holiday meal
> a favorite holiday decoration
> a gift they would like to receive
> a gift they would like to give

Christmas Tree

Materials

construction paper—
8½″ × 11″ green, small
pieces or scraps of several
colors

pencil, scissors, glue,
crayons

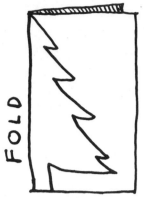

Procedure
Have each student:

- Fold the green paper in half with the longer edges together.

- Draw one side of the tree outline as shown.

- Cut out the tree.

- Decorate the tree by making ornaments and trimmings
  with scraps of paper, or draw them with crayons.

Handy Wreath

Materials

construction paper— six
sheets (for each student)
of 8½″ × 11″ green, one
sheet 5½″ × 8½″ red

pencil, scissors, glue

Procedure
Have each student:

- Fold one piece of green paper
  in half with the shorter edges
  together. Draw lines as shown
  to cut a ring.

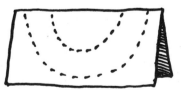

- Cut out and unfold the ring.

- Fold each of the other five sheets of green paper in half
  with the shorter edges together.

- Trace one hand on each folded paper.

- Cut out the hands on each folded sheet. (There should be ten hands when the cutting is completed. These hand-shaped pieces of paper will be the "leaves" of the wreath.)

- Glue all the leaves around the ring.

- Cut a bow and some berries from the red paper. Glue them on the wreath.

Cover That Sneeze

Materials
paper—8½″ × 11″ manila; 8½″ × 11″ pink, tan, brown, or black construction paper

facial tissues, pencil, crayons, glue

Procedure
Have each student:

- Draw and color a large face to fill most of the manila paper.

- Trace one hand and wrist on the construction paper.

- Cut on the lines of the tracing.

- Glue the tissue near the nose on the face of the drawing. (Only a small amount of glue is needed.)

- Glue the hand over the tissue with the bottom edge of the wrist along the bottom edge of the manila paper as shown.

Valentine Greeting Card

Materials
paper—8½″ × 11″ red or pink construction paper, 5½″ × 8½″ white duplicating paper

scissors, glue, crayons

Procedure
Have each student:

- Cut a snowflake or heart from the white duplicating paper.

- Fold the red construction paper in half with the shorter sides together to make a card.

- Glue the white snowflake or heart on the front of the card.

- Write a valentine message inside.

Valentine Butterfly

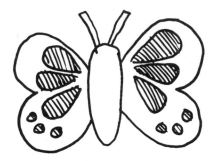

Materials
construction paper—8½″ × 11″ red, small pieces of several other colors

pencil, scissors, glue

Procedure
Have each student:

- Fold the red construction paper in half with the shorter edges together.

- Draw a large heart on one side of the folded sheet. Fill up the paper.

- Cut on the lines of the heart. There should be two hearts of the same size.

- Use the scraps of the red paper to cut a long, narrow oval for the butterfly body.

- Glue the wings behind the butterfly body.

- Cut two narrow strips from the scraps of construction paper. Glue them to the top of the body to form antennae.

- Cut small shapes from different colors of construction paper. Glue the shapes on the wings.

Valentine Messenger

Materials

construction paper—
8½″ × 11″ red, 4¼″ × 11″
white, scraps of different
colors

scissors, glue

Procedure

Have each student:

- Cut one large red heart and one medium-size red heart. Glue them together as shown.

- Cut four small red hearts from the remaining pieces of red paper.

- Cut four strips of white paper. Fold each strip accordion-style. (Do this by folding back and forth until the entire length of the strip is used.)

- Glue the strips behind the larger red heart (body) to form arms and legs.

- Glue one small red heart to the end of each accordion-folded white strip to form hands and feet.

- Cut out facial features and decorative trim such as neckties, bows, or buttons from the scraps of brightly colored construction paper.

- Glue the features and trimmings on the valentine messenger.

Shamrock Rubbings

Materials

1 tagboard shamrock pattern (approximately 3" wide) for each student

8½" × 11" manila paper

crayons

Procedure

Have each student:

- Place the shamrock pattern underneath the manila paper.

- Hold the paper tightly so the shamrock does not slide.

- Color back and forth over the pattern until the entire outline of the shamrock is visible.

- Move the pattern to a new position under the paper and make a different rubbing.

- Repeat this process until the manila paper is filled with a shamrock-rubbing design.

Lucky Potato Person

Materials

six to eight 3" tagboard shamrock patterns

construction paper—
8½" × 11" green, 5½" × 8½" tan

pencil, scissors, glue, crayons

Procedure

Have each student:

- Cut an oval from the tan paper to make a potato head.

- Fold the green paper in half with the shorter edges together. Cut it into two parts along the fold line.

- Cut a top hat from one of the pieces of green paper.

- Trace the shamrock pattern twice on the other piece of green paper. Pass the pattern to a neighbor.

- Cut out the two shamrocks.

- Cut two triangles and a small circle from the rest of the green paper.

- Glue the hat on the top of the potato head.

- Glue the shamrocks to the head just below the hat; they will be the puffs of hair.

- Glue the triangles and the circle together to form a bow tie at the bottom of the potato head.

- Add facial features with crayons.

Vase and Flowers

Materials
paper—8½″ × 11″ white construction paper, 4¼″ × 5½″ tissue or crepe paper in four or five colors

pencil, crayons, glue

Procedure
Have each student:

- Place the paper vertically.

- Draw and color a vase on the lower half of the paper.

- Draw four to five green stems and leaves protruding from the vase.

- Crush the small pieces of colored tissue or crepe paper.

- Glue the crushed paper wads to the ends of the stems.

Kites

Materials
8½″ × 11″ white
construction paper
6″ segment of yarn
ruler, pencil, crayons,
scissors, glue

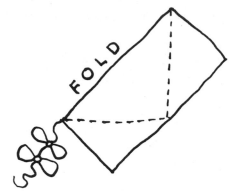

Procedure
Have each student:

- Fold the paper in half with the longer edges together.

- Fold the paper in half again, this time with the shorter edges together. Then reopen to the first lengthwise fold.

- Make a pencil mark at the point on the unfolded edge where the crease was made.

- Use a ruler to draw a pencil line from the upper corner on the fold to the pencil mark. Draw a second line from the lower corner on the fold to the pencil mark on the unfolded edge.

- Cut on the pencil lines. Do not cut on the fold.

- Open the paper. Decorate the kite.

- Cut bows for the tail of the kite from the scraps. Glue them on the yarn.

- Glue the tail to the back of the kite.

Mother's Day Greetings

Materials

construction paper—
8½″ × 11″ white, yellow,
or pink

pencil, scissors, crayons

Procedure

Have each student:

- Fold the paper in half with the shorter edges together.

- Hold the fold and cut one triangle from the center of the folded side as shown.

- Cut two right triangles from the unfolded side as shown.

- Decorate the card with crayons. Write a Mother's Day greeting inside the card.

LANGUAGE ARTS

Language arts activities reinforce listening, speaking, reading, and writing. Most of the activities can be adjusted to suit different grade and ability levels.

The first three activities will work best with small groups and thus are called Reading Group Games. The next set of activities is designed for larger groups and is called Class Games. In these two groups the focus is on listening, speaking, and reading.

The third group is called Writing Activities. As you would expect, the activities focus on writing. For these exercises, you might spend time with pre-writing motivation—brainstorming, discussion, examples, practice. After the writing is completed, the students often enjoy sharing their work.

For more activities that engage students in writing, see the Resource Guide on page 104. *Writing Well, Reaching for Language Creativity,* and *Think! Draw! Write!* are three helpful resources for creative writing.

READING GROUP GAMES

Three-in-a-Row Bingo

Materials
ten to twelve slips of paper

chalkboard, chalk, pencil

Procedure
- Write a different letter or word on each slip of paper. Choose the letters or words from reading lessons.

- Draw two nine-square bingo cards on the chalkboard. Write a different word or letter in each square. Use the same words or letters as those on the slips of paper. Arrange the words or letters differently on each bingo card.

- Choose one student to pick the slips of paper out of the box and read them to the players.

- Divide the remaining group members into two teams.

- Send a student from each team to the chalkboard. Then have the reader pick a slip of paper from the box and name the letter or word. The team players use chalk to mark an X on the bingo card space that has the same letter or word.

- Send the next two players to the chalkboard, and continue the game in this manner.

- The team that gets three X marks in a row is the winner.

- Reshuffle the slips of paper, choose a new reader, and play another round.

Apples and Ladders

Materials

chalkboard, chalk

vocabulary words from reading lessons

Procedure

- Draw the apple tree and two ladders on the chalkboard as shown.

- Write a word on each rung of the ladders.

- Tell the students they can become "climbers" as they read the words on the ladders.

- Direct each student to read the words on the rungs.

- Every student who correctly reads all the words may draw an apple on the tree and write his or her name on the apple.

Word-Hunt Relay

Materials
chalkboard, chalk

Procedure

- Divide the reading group into two or three teams, depending on the size of the group.

- Write a short list of consonants or blends on the chalkboard.

- Tell the students to think of a word that begins with one of the letters or blends on the chalkboard. The words must be names of things that can be found in the classroom.

- Send the first player on each team to the chalkboard to write a word.

- Have each player pass the chalk to the next player to continue the relay. Students may help one another. Spellings must be correct.

- The first team to write words for all the letters and spell all the words correctly is the winner.

Variation
For each successive round, change the categories of words. Possible categories include things for cooking, sports equipment, things for lunch, items in a grocery store.

CLASS GAMES

Spreading Rumors

Materials
ten slips of paper, pencil

Procedure
- Write five brief descriptive messages on separate slips of paper. Make a second copy of each message. A sample message is: "Six children were playing quietly outside. Mother heard a child shout. Sally had fallen off the seesaw."

- Divide the class into two teams. Arrange each team in a circle.

- Give the first student on each team a slip of paper with a message written on it. Both teams should have the same message.

- Allow enough time for each first player to read the message, and then take away the slips of paper.

- Direct each student to whisper the message to the player seated to the right. That player repeats the message to the next player, and so on.

- The last student on each team repeats the message aloud.

- Compare the final versions of the messages with the original version written on the two slips of paper.

- The team that maintains the most similarity to the original version scores a point. After a total of five rounds of different messages, the team with the higher number of points wins.

More sample messages:
Mary Smith came home and saw her back door open. She wondered what had wandered inside. Her black dog was barking. A circus monkey was in the kitchen.

A tall man with a tan trench coat walked into the flower shop. He ordered six bunches of zinnias. Then he put all the flowers in one sack.

Storytelling

Materials
none

Procedure

- Start a story with an interesting sentence.

- Have each student continue the story in turn by adding another sentence. The goal is to complete the story in exactly one round of the class.

Trains of Thought

Materials
paper, pencil, chalkboard, chalk

Procedure

- Explain the concept of a series of word associations—a train of thought. Demonstrate with an example such as: mail—envelope—letter—write—pen—ink—black.

- Write a word on the chalkboard and begin gathering words for the train. Use a volunteer system, or have students answer in sequence.

- Write each new word on the chalkboard.

- Review each completed chain and discuss how each word leads to the next.

- Continue in this manner for several rounds.

- Write a word on the chalkboard and have each student write an individual train of thought on paper.

- Allow volunteers to read their lists and explain their thinking patterns.

Alphabet Lineup

Materials
3″ × 5″ index cards with words written on them—possibly words from spelling, science, or reading lessons

Procedure
- Divide the class into groups of five or six students.
- Distribute the word cards, one to each student.
- Tell students to keep their words secret until their group's turn arises.
- In turn, each group moves to the front of the room, and the students arrange themselves in alphabetical order according to the words on their cards. Once they are in progress, group members may help one another.
- Time each group. The group with a correct alphabetization in the shortest amount of time is the winner.
- To make the game more challenging, give each group a set of words that begin with the same letter.

Sames and Opposites

Materials
a list of words that have both synonyms and antonyms

chalkboard, chalk

Procedure
- Divide the class into two teams. Briefly review the meanings of *synonyms* and *antonyms*.
- Draw a chart on the chalkboard as shown.
- Write one of the words on your list in the first space of row one.

Word	Synonym	Antonym

- Send the first player on each team to the chart on the chalkboard.

- The player on team A writes a synonym in the appropriate column, and the player from team B writes an antonym.

Completed Chart

Word	Synonym	Antonym
sick	ill	healthy
help	aid	harm

- For each next word, have the teams alternate their responses from synonyms to antonyms.

- Teams earn a point for each correct response.

Adjective Chain Game

Materials
list of nouns, for example: jacket, tree, house, hat, ice cream
chalkboard, chalk, paper, pencil

Procedure
- Write a list of nouns on the chalkboard.

- Divide the class into two teams.

- Team A starts. The first student chooses a noun and then names an adjective to modify it, for example, *jacket—large.*

- The next player on team A gives another adjective, and so on, until any player repeats an adjective or is unable to think of an adjective within ten to fifteen seconds.

- Keep a written record of the adjectives given. The number of adjectives is the score for the first round for team A.

- Team B takes its turn. The first student on team B chooses a different noun and gives an adjective. The game continues in this manner.

Noun	Adjectives
school	big fun quiet

- At the end of three to four rounds, the team with the higher score wins.

Categories

Materials
none

Procedure

- Choose a word or words that can be the title of a category, such as countries, states, games, things that grow, or things that are small.

- Divide the class into two teams. The first student of team A begins by naming a word that will fit the category. For the category *countries,* a word could be *Peru.*

- The first student on team B must give a word that fits the category and begins with the last letter of the word just named. For the word *Peru,* the next response would be *Uruguay.*

- Alternate between teams. The students on each team must answer in turn. Award two points for each correct answer.

- When a student cannot answer or answers incorrectly, score one point for the opposing team.

- When a chain can no longer be continued by either team, choose a new category and begin another round.

- The team with the higher number of points at the end of an even number of rounds is the winner.

Boiler Burst

Materials
small slips of paper—at least one per student

pencil

Procedure

- Write a story fill-in on each slip of paper. (For Super Bowl and Baseball Boiler Bursts, the story fill-in that names your home team will be the key name, so be sure that you do not write the key name on a slip of paper.)

- Give each student a slip of paper that has a story fill-in written on it. (Doubles of the story fill-ins can be used if the class is large.)

- Tell the students to listen to the story. Explain that when you pause for a blank, each student in turn will say a story fill-in.

- Tell the class the key name for the story that you will read. Explain that every time they hear the key name they are to change seats.

- Read the story. Pause for each blank so a student can say a story fill-in to fill the blank. Pencil in the story fill-ins as they are given.

- After all the story blanks have been filled in, reread the story to the class without the seat-change action.

Halloween Hobgoblin Boiler Burst

Key name: Halloween Hobgoblin

Story fill-ins:

screechy owl	rickety broom
rusty gate	crackling thunder
ghoulish ghost	haunted house
horrible hyena	creaking door
wicked old witch	fat black cat
howling dog	menacing monster
giant bats	jagged lightning
scary black spider	

Once upon a time there was a *Halloween Hobgoblin* who lived in a ___ on a high hill. He had lots of friends, including the ___ , the ___ , and the ___ . One dark Halloween night, he flew through the sky on his ___ . He was looking for a ___ . He stopped at the house of his friend, the ___ . In a very spooky voice, the *Halloween Hobgoblin* asked for a ___ to eat.

The ___ said, "I don't have a ___ , but I do have a terrific ___ . Would you like it?"

"I believe I would," replied the *Halloween Hobgoblin*. "And then later I will find my friend, the ___ ."

(Continued on next page.)

The ___ started howling outside, and a ___ flew by the window.

"My, what a wonderful night!" said the *Halloween Hobgoblin*. "Would you like another ___ ?" asked the ___ .

The *Halloween Hobgoblin* replied, "No, thanks," and he flew away on his ___ with a ___ following behind. The moon looked like a ___ that night. In the sky were a ___ and a ___ .

The flying friends came to a big, old house that was falling apart. They opened the door and walked inside. There was a surprise Halloween party going on! All of the *Halloween Hobgoblin*'s friends were there. He saw ___ , ___ , ___ , and ___ . What fun they had as they danced to "The Monster Mash"! The *Halloween Hobgoblin* walked up the dark, creaky stairs to look for a ___ . At the top of the stairs he met a ___ .

As the clock struck midnight, the *Halloween Hobgoblin* squealed, "It's time for me to hurry back to my ___ ." So off he flew on his ___ with his friend, the ___ , trailing behind. They flew happily home to their ___ . It was fun to talk about all the fun they had had that Halloween.

Super Bowl Boiler Burst

Key name: use the name of your local team

Story fill-ins:

Bears	Chargers	49ers	Raiders
Bengals	Chiefs	Giants	Rams
Bills	Colts	Jets	Redskins
Broncos	Cowboys	Lions	Saints
Browns	Dolphins	Oilers	Seahawks
Buccaneers	Eagles	Packers	Steelers
Cardinals	Falcons	Patriots	Vikings

Time surely flies! Super Bowl Fifty was played yesterday, and what a crazy game it was! The crowd at the stadium was full of ＿＿ and ＿＿ . The (*key name*) were playing the ＿＿ . In the stadium, the people were cheering like ＿＿ . Everyone hoped for a good game.

The (*key name*) rode into the stadium on the backs of the ＿＿ . The team was full of energy. For lunch they had eaten ＿＿ and ＿＿ . They had wrestled their friends the ＿＿ . Now they looked like ＿＿ and they were ready to play the ＿＿ .

To the surprise of everyone, instead of kicking the ball, the (*key name*) tackled the ＿＿ to start the game. The ＿＿ in the stands cheered loudly. Some people turned cartwheels with the ＿＿ . The ＿＿ and ＿＿ played so well that the (*key name*) asked for extra time. They wanted to score more touchdowns.

This time they kicked the ＿＿ instead of the ball. Someone in the crowd remarked that this game wasn't much like the Super Bowl she remembered from twenty years ago.

Just then the ＿＿ started howling and some ＿＿ flew over the stadium. The sky was filled with ＿＿ . Everyone tried to catch one. This caused quite a delay, so the ＿＿ and the ＿＿ played Monopoly with the ＿＿ and the ＿＿ .

While all this was happening, the ＿＿ threw a pass and hit a flock of ＿＿ . The (*key name*) ran fifteen yards and scored another touchdown. Meanwhile the crowd cheered the ＿＿ as they turned somersaults around the ＿＿ .

Still playing the game, the (*key name*) scored again, grabbed a fumble, and scored again! The game was wild by then! "Let's wipe out those ＿＿ and score more touch-downs!" the (*key name*) called. What an unusual event!

When the game was over and the (*key name*) had won, the team flew back home. They were greeted by the ＿＿ . Super Bowl Fifty was terrific, everyone agreed. Next year the (*key name*) will play the ＿＿ , and surely the ＿＿ will be there. These football games may be different from those of years ago, but they certainly are entertaining!

Baseball Boiler Burst

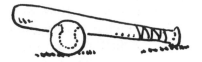

Key name: use the name of your local team

Story fill-ins:

Angels	Cubs	Orioles	Royals
Astros	Dodgers	Padres	Tigers
Athletics	Expos	Phillies	Twins
Blue Jays	Giants	Pirates	White Sox
Braves	Indians	Rangers	Yankees
Brewers	Mariners	Reds	
Cardinals	Mets	Red Sox	

It's springtime! It's the season for picnics, flowers, and (*key name*)! Last week in a huge stadium, several games of baseball were played. In one game the (*key name*) were playing the ___ . The crowd was full of ___ and ___ . They were as excited as nervous ___ .

The pitcher for the ___ threw the ball. He hit the ___ and then ran to the ___ in the stands. The crowd cheered and cheered at this unusual behavior. The mascot for the ___ was jumping wildly. He was even dancing on the dugout of the ___ . All the players in the outfield looked like ___ and played like ___ . Through all the commotion, the (*key name*) were awesome!

The games grew more exciting. Soon the crowd was cheering for the ___ and the ___ . One by one, the ___ were dropping like ___ . The ___ scored many runs, and the ___ were losing. In the best game the (*key name*) had scored two runs. When it was time for the ___ to bat, the weather changed suddenly. It began to rain ___ and ___ .

During the rain delay some of the ___ serenaded the ___ .
Then everyone sang "Take Me Out to the Ball Game."
The ___ did a sun dance. Soon the sun came out and the
___ , ___ , ___ , and ___ returned to the field to continue
their games. In the best game, the batters for the ___ went
down in order. Then the (*key name*) came to bat. It was
the ninth inning; the score was tied, and the bases were
loaded. Suddenly the best batter hit a grand-slam home
run. The (*key name*) won the game!

After such a series of vigorous games, all the teams headed
into the clubhouse for lunch. The ___ were the hosts. They
had planned a menu of ___ and ___ . The ___ and the ___
were the guests of honor. As the teams ate lunch they talked
about the silly day. But the happy (*key name*) thought
about their next game.

WRITING ACTIVITIES

Sticker Stories

Materials
writing paper, practice paper

pencil, decorative stickers (at least one for each student)

Procedure
- Allow students to select stickers for their stories.

- Have the students stick their stickers on the top of their writing papers.

- Direct the students to write interesting stories using the practice paper. The stories should include the characters or scenes depicted in the stickers.

- When a student's practice story is written well enough to be considered the final version, it can be copied onto the writing paper that has the sticker on it.

Silly Rhymes

Materials
paper, pencil, chalkboard, chalk

Procedure
- Discuss rhyming words. Show that rhyming words can be used to make humorous poems.

- Write this example on the chalkboard.
    As I was walking down the lane,
    I met a twelve-foot purple crane.

- Have the students identify the rhyming words in the example. Point out the placement of the words *lane* and *crane*.

- Direct the students to make a short list of rhyming words.

- From their lists, have them choose some rhyming words and write short silly rhymes.

Cinquains

Materials

paper, pencil

Procedure

- Explain that a cinquain is a five-line poem with a specific structure.

- Read a cinquain to the students. Here is an example:

    Teacher
    Helpful and kind
    Laughing, caring, teaching
    Ready to work so I can learn
    My friend

- Explain the structure:

    Line 1—two syllables (naming the subject)
    Line 2—four syllables (describing the subject)
    Line 3—six syllables (expressing action)
    Line 4—eight syllables (expressing a feeling or idea)
    Line 5—two syllables (another name for the subject)

- With input from students, make a list of topics for cinquains.

- Direct the students to write cinquains.

- Allow time for volunteers to share their poems.

Story Situations

Materials
paper, pencil

Procedure
- Present a situation and direct the students to write a paragraph or a short story.

Here are some sample situations:

> A clown on the corner is giving away baby elephants to good caretakers. You want to take one home. Write a paragraph to convince your parents that you should have one.

> Imagine you are taking a trip backward in time. Write about one of your adventures.

> Imagine that you are a miniperson from the land of Teeny Weeny. You are sitting on the windowsill of your living room. Describe your appearance and the appearance of the room as a miniperson would see it.

> A bandit just came running out of the bank with a bag of money almost too heavy to carry. Write what you plan to do about the bandit and an adventure that you have as a result of your plan.

> You wake up on Halloween morning and discover that you have turned into a black cat. What do your parents and friends say? Tell about an adventure you (as the cat) have.

> You are stranded on an island and you want some help. Write a note that could be placed in a bottle. Describe what you plan to do while you wait for a reply.

Shape Stories

Materials

8½″ × 11″ construction paper—colors may vary

student writing paper

stapler, scissors, pencil, chalkboard, chalk

Procedure

- Prepare paper forms by cutting out specific shapes from the construction paper. The shapes may be determined by the writing topics. For instance, a barnyard story might be written on a pig shape.

- Cut out a smaller size of the same shape from the writing paper. Staple the writing paper on top of the construction paper shape.

- Prepare the students for writing. Engage them in brain-storming about the shapes—topics, key words, related ideas.

- List the ideas on the chalkboard.

- Have each student write a paragraph or short story on practice paper.

- When a student's story is written well enough to be considered the final version, it can be copied onto the writing paper shape.

Note: For more activities like this one, try the books *Shape-a-Story* and *Shape-a-Poem*. See the Resource Guide on page 104 for details.

Letter Writing

Materials
paper, pencil,
chalkboard, chalk

Procedure

- Review the basic parts of a friendly letter.

- Assign a topic or allow the students to select their own topics.

- Have students write letters and use their own names as the signatures.

- Topic selections may be written on the chalkboard. Here are some suggestions:

> Nursery rhyme advice letters in response to a given situation, for example: Dear Helpful Student, My little kittens are always losing their mittens. What should I do?

> Thank you letters in response to home or school activities

> Fantasy letters—to fictional or historic characters

> Get well letters—perhaps to the regular teacher

> Animal complaints, for example: turtle complains about the expression "slow as a turtle," mouse complains about "quiet as a mouse"

MATHEMATICS

These math activities are simple, instructional, and enjoyable. They require very few materials—usually only paper and pencil, chalkboard, or flash cards. The most simple activities are presented first, and the complexity increases gradually. Skill areas include number recognition, basic facts, computation, and estimation.

You can adjust the levels of difficulty by changing the math operations of an activity, for instance, from addition to multiplication. Most of the activities are team games. Students will enjoy the drill minus the drudgery.

Fire Fighter, Fire Fighter

Materials
chalkboard, chalk

Procedure

- Draw the smoking house, numbered ladder, and the fire company roster on the chalkboard as shown.

- Choose a student to be the first fire fighter who will "climb" the ladder.

- Have the student read the numerals on each rung of the ladder.

- Direct the remaining students to read the numerals in turn.

- As the students correctly identify all the numerals, they may print their names on the fire company roster.

- Change the numerals for successive rounds. To increase the difficulty, print addition or subtraction problems on the rungs of the ladder.

Jump the Answer

Materials
Flash cards

Procedure
- Show and read aloud selected flash cards of addition or subtraction facts.
- Give each student a chance to "jump" the answers to one or two flash cards. For example, for a flash card that has 5 + 1, the student would jump six times.
- If the student jumps correctly, he or she may flash the next card to the next student.
- Rotate until everyone has had at least one chance to jump an answer.

Number Bounce

Materials
rubber playground ball

Procedure
- Choose one student to be the "bouncer."
- Have the student bounce the ball a certain number of times, for example, a number between one and ten.
- The bouncer must then call on a class member to tell how many times the ball was bounced.
- If the student answers correctly, he or she becomes the next bouncer.

Switch Seats

Materials
none

Procedure

- Begin the activity with a practice session. Use ordinal numbers to direct specific students to switch seats. "The first person in the third row switches with the second person in the fourth row."

- After one or two rounds of practice, choose a student to be the first leader.

- Explain the challenge of the game: after the direction to switch seats is given, the leader will try to steal the seat of one of the switching players.

- The student who is left without the seat is the next leader.

- Play a number of rounds. Encourage students to involve all their classmates in at least one directed switch.

Flash Card Numbers Change

Materials
flash cards with sums from one to ten

two or three sets of cards numbered from one to ten

Procedure

- Arrange the students in a circle.

- Distribute the cards in random numerical order, one per student.

- Choose a student leader to begin the game.

- Direct the leader to show and read a flash card to the class.

- The students who have the number cards with the correct answer must trade seats. The leader tries to steal one of the seats.

- The student who is without a seat is the next leader.

Sharks and Minnows

Materials
chalkboard, chalk, flash cards

Procedure
- Draw two sharks and ten small fish on the chalkboard.
- Divide the class into two teams. Identify five fish for one team and five fish for the other.
- Show flash cards to the students, alternating between teams.
- Each player must answer without assistance.
- For every three correct answers, one team member may erase one of the opposing team's fish.
- The first team that eats all the opponents' fish is the winner.

Tens and Ones

Materials
chalkboard, chalk

Procedure

Tens	Ones	
2	3	=23
4	2	=42
3	7	=37

- Draw the place value chart on the chalkboard as shown.
- Make a statement to the class such as, "I am thinking of a number that is two tens and three ones. What is the number?"
- Choose a volunteer to answer the questions by completing the appropriate spaces in the chart on the chalkboard.
- If the student is correct, he or she may make the next place value statement and choose the next volunteer to answer.

Addition Relay

Materials
chalkboard, chalk

Procedure

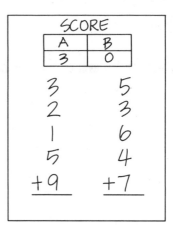

- Divide the class into teams of five to six persons.

- On a cue such as "go," the first student on each team moves to the chalkboard, writes a number, and passes the chalk to the next player.

- This next player moves to the chalkboard and repeats the process. The relay continues in this manner until the last student on the team moves to the chalkboard.

- The last players must add all the numbers that have been written by their teammates.

- Score one point for correct addition. Score an additional point for the team that finishes its addition first.

- Play for five or six rounds, or until every person on the teams has had a chance to add a column of numbers.

- The team that earns the highest score is the winner.

Note: Remind the students to write their numbers in columns and to write legibly.

Around the World

Materials
addition or subtraction flash cards

Procedure

- Direct the students to sit in a circle. Choose one student to be the first traveler.

- Have the traveler stand behind one child in the circle.

- Present an addition or subtraction flash card to these two students.

- The two students tell the answer to the flash card as quickly as possible.

- Whoever answers correctly first moves on to the next student in the circle. The one who answered last remains in that space. If the students tie, present another flash card until the tie is broken.

- If the time permits, play around the circle at least twice.

Chalkboard Baseball

Materials
chalkboard, chalk, list of math problems

Procedure

- Divide the class into two teams.

- Direct one team to choose a catcher and the other to choose a batter. The catcher and the batter stand with their backs to the chalkboard.

- Write a math problem on the chalkboard, omitting answer.

- On the signal "batter up," both players turn to the chalkboard and call out the answer. If the catcher answers first, the batter is out and the next batter is up. After three outs, the next team is up to bat.

- If the batter correctly answers the problem first, score a run for the team.

- Play until everyone has had a chance at the chalkboard.

- After an even number of innings, the team with the higher score is the winner.

Chalk Tray Race

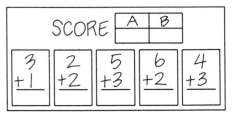

Materials
chalkboard with chalk tray, chalk, flash cards

Procedure

- Divide the class into two teams.

- Choose two students, one from each team, to start the game.

- Direct the two students to stand at opposite ends of the chalk tray. They should stand with their backs to the chalkboard.

- Place flash cards in a row along the chalk tray.

- At a given signal, the students turn around to face the chalkboard and begin to write the answers to the flash cards above the cards. They work toward each other until they meet.

- Score one point for each correct answer for each student.

- Continue in this manner until every player has had a chance at the chalkboard.

- Total the points for each team. The team with the higher score wins.

Outdoor Math Call Ball

Materials
rubber playground ball

Procedure

- Have the students stand in a circle on the playground.

- Choose one student to be the caller.

- The student caller stands in the center of the circle and holds the ball.

- The caller calls out an addition or subtraction combination and names a student. For example, "4 + 2, Sandy!"

- The student whose name has been called must give the answer and grab the ball before it bounces once. If successful, he or she becomes the next caller.

Racetrack Math

START→

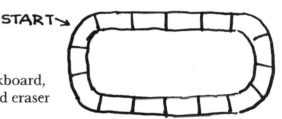

Materials
flash cards, chalkboard, chalk, chalkboard eraser

Procedure

- Divide the class into two teams. Label one team X and the other O.

- Draw the racetrack on the chalkboard as shown.

- Show a flash card to the first student on team X. On a correct answer, the student marks the team symbol, X, in the first section of the racetrack. No mark is made if the answer is incorrect.

- Show a flash card to the first student on team O. Again, a correct answer earns a mark on the racetrack.

- Alternate between teams as you flash the cards. Students with correct responses should erase their team's mark and make a new mark in the next section of the racetrack.

- The team that circles the racetrack first is the winner.

All in a Row

Materials
8½″ × 11″ white
duplicating paper

pencil, buttons, tokens,
or small pieces of paper
to mark a bingo card

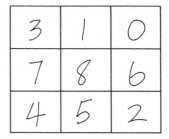

Procedure
Have each student:

- Fold the paper into thirds. Then, keeping the paper folded, fold it into thirds again.

- Unfold the entire paper—there should be nine sections.

- Write any nine digits, 0-9, a different digit in each section.

Then:

- Give sample word problems such as:

    Judy has three marbles. Diane has five more marbles than Judy. How many marbles does Diane have?

- Direct the students to check their bingo cards and to cover the number that answers the problem.

- When a player has covered three numbers in a row, he or she calls "Bingo!"

- Play several rounds as time permits.

One, Two, Buzz

Materials
none

Procedure
- Decide on a counting pattern and a pattern for substituting the word *buzz*. For example:

    even numbers—one, *buzz*, three, *buzz*, five, *buzz*, and so on.

    multiples of three—one, two, *buzz*, four, five, *buzz*, seven, eight, *buzz*, and so on.

- Have students count in sequence around the room and substitute *buzz* for the appropriate numbers according to the selected pattern.

Guestimation

Materials
teacher-made flash cards showing addition or subtraction of large numbers

Procedure
- Divide the class into two teams.
- Tell the students that they will have ten seconds to estimate the sums or differences of the two numbers shown on a flash card.
- Show a flash card to the first two players.
- After the students give their estimates, determine who is closer to the actual answer. The student whose answer is closer earns a point for his or her team.
- Play until each team member has had a chance to make an estimate. The team with the higher score wins the game.

Quiz Down

 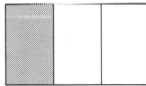

Materials
fraction flash cards

Procedure
- Divide the class into two teams.
- Select a student leader to flash the cards, or plan to flash them yourself.
- The leader flashes a card and asks the first person on one of the teams to name the fractional part.
- If the student answers correctly, the team earns a point. If the student answers incorrectly, the opposing team gets a chance to give the correct answer and earn a point.
- Alternate between teams. At the end of three or four rounds, the team with more points is the winner.

Magic Math

Materials
chalkboard, chalk, paper, pencil

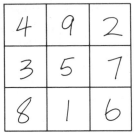

Procedure
- On the chalkboard, draw a large square with nine empty blocks.

- Direct the students to copy the square on their papers.

- Have them arrange the digits 1–9 in the blocks so that each row, column, and diagonal adds up to fifteen. Each number can be used only once.

Magic Wheel

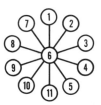

Materials
chalkboard, chalk, paper, pencil

Procedure
- On the chalkboard, draw five lines that cross at one center point. Make a circle at the end of each line and one around the center point.

- Tell students to copy the drawing on their papers.

- Direct the students to write numbers from one to eleven in the circles so that the total of all three numbers on every line equals eighteen.

- Each number, 1–11, may be used only once.

Magic Triangle

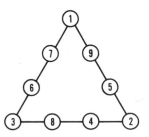

Materials
chalkboard, chalk, paper, pencil

Procedure
- On the chalkboard, draw an equilateral triangle that has a circle at each point and two circles on each side.

- Tell students to copy the drawing on their papers.

- Direct the students to write the numbers from one to nine in the circles so that the sum of the numbers along each side equals seventeen.

- Each digit, 1–9, may be used only once.

Follow the Signs

Materials
chalkboard, chalk, paper, pencil

Procedure

- On the chalkboard, draw the chart as shown.

- Direct the students to copy the chart on their papers.

- Tell the students to work the computations by following the operational signs across the top row of the chart.

- When the chart is completed across each row, all the answers are to be totaled in the bottom row.

	x 3	+5	−2	
3				
2				
5				
8				
1				
totals				

Completed Chart

	x 3	+5	−2	
3	9	14	12	
2	6	11	9	
5	15	20	18	
8	24	29	27	
1	3	8	6	
totals	57	82	72	211

Mental Chains

Materials
paper, pencil

Procedure

- Dictate problems to the students and have them work the computations mentally. They are to write only their final answers.

  Here are some sample problems:

  Start with thirty-six. Add four. Subtract one. Add twenty. What is the answer?

  Start with twenty. Add five. Subtract three. Add ten. What is the answer?

Multiplication Relay

Materials
chalkboard, chalk, pencil,
paper

Procedure

- Distribute a blank sheet of paper to the first student in each row.

- Explain that each row of students is a separate team and each team will be assigned a number as a multiplier.

- Write the multiplier for each team on the chalkboard.

- Then announce a number. The first student on each team multiplies that announced number by the team multiplier, does the work on the paper, and passes the paper to the second student in the row.

- The second student in the row multiplies the first student's answer by the team multiplier. This process continues down the row.

- The first row that finishes the multiplication computations correctly wins the relay.

Row 1 Team 4	Row 2 Team 6	Row 3 Team 3
3 ×4	2 ×6	5 ×3
12 ×4	12 ×6	15 ×3
48 ×4	72 ×6	45 ×3
192 ×4	432 ×6	135 ×3
768	2592	405

Multiplication Table Fold-Up

Materials
8½″ × 11″ duplicating paper

chalkboard, chalk, pencil

Procedure
On the chalkboard, copy the chart as shown and write numbers across the top row and along the left columns. Then have each student:

X	6	7	8
3	18	21	24
4	24	28	32
5	30	35	40

- Fold the paper in half with the longer sides together.

- Fold the paper in half again, this time with the shorter sides together.

- Fold the paper in half two more times, first with the longer sides together and then with the shorter sides together.

- Open the folded paper. There should be sixteen sections.

- Copy the numbers from the chalkboard into the corresponding sections on the chart.

- Complete the chart by multiplying the numbers as on a multiplication table.

Upset the Product Pot

Materials
multiplication flash cards

small slips of paper (at least one per student), pencil

Procedure

- Write one multiplication product on each slip of paper. (A completed multiplication table is a convenient source for the products.)

- Distribute the slips of paper, one to each student.

- Select one student to be the first flash card caller. This student stands in front of the class.

- Remove one student seat from the playing area.

- Have the flash card caller show a flash card and call out the problem.

- The student in the playing area who has the product stands to tell the answer. If correct, the student stands behind the caller. If incorrect, the student sits down. If more than one student calls the answer, the first to give the correct answer should stand behind the caller, and the second student should sit down.

- When the student caller has a majority of students standing, he or she calls "Upset the product pot!" At this signal everyone, including the caller, hurries to a new seat.

- The student who is left without a seat becomes the next caller, and the game continues.

This Is Your Number

Materials
paper, pencil

Procedure

- Explain to the students that they are to follow your oral directions and work the computations on their papers. Then, after hearing their results, you will be able to identify their original numbers, unless they have calculated incorrectly.

- Read these directions:
  Select any number greater than zero.
  Multiply that number by three.
  Now add one.
  Multiply this number by three.
  Now add your original number.

- Have volunteers give their final totals.

- Mentally remove the final digit of each answer. The remaining digit or digits will be the original number. Note the example:
  Select a number: 8
  $8 \times 3 = 24$
  $24 + 1 = 25$
  $25 \times 3 = 75$
  $75 + 8 = 83$
  Remove the 3 and the result is 8, the original number.

I'll Guess Your Age and Birth Month

Materials
paper, pencil,
chalkboard, chalk

Procedure

- Have the students follow your oral directions and complete the computations on paper.

- Read these directions:

    Counting the months by numbers, write the number of your birth month on your paper.

    Multiply that number by two.

    Add five to the product.

    Multiply that number by fifty.

    Now add your age.

    Subtract three hundred sixty-five.

    Add one hundred fifteen.

- Final answers will vary, but if the computations are correct, the final number will show the number of the month the student was born and the student's age. Note this example of a twelve-year-old born in December.

    December = 12

    $12 \times 2 = 24$

    $24 + 5 = 29$

    $29 \times 50 = 1450$

    $1450 + 12 = 1462$

    $1462 - 365 = 1097$

    $1097 + 115 = 1212$

    1212 shows the number of the month of December (12) and the student's age (12).

- Have students volunteer their final answers. Write the numbers on the chalkboard and tell them their ages and months of birth. If a response you give is incorrect, tell the student to check for an error in the computations.

INDOOR GAMES

These games are challenging and competitive, yet they can be played in the regular classroom. Students enjoy participating in games that are not related to school subjects.

The games in this section are easy to manage in enclosed spaces such as a classroom. Many of the games give students a chance to move about without encouraging chaotic excitement. These games help youngsters stretch a bit within a short period of time. You'll find that all the games in this section work well when the students need a quick boost of energy.

Another resource for indoor activities is *Incredible Indoor Games*. See the Resource Guide for a description.

Flannel Board Memory Game

Materials
flannel board, felt shapes

Procedure

- Choose a student to place four to six felt shapes on the flannel board.

- The student then tells the class what has been done. For example, "I have picked a circle, a square, a triangle, and a rectangle. They are in a line on the board."

- Direct the students to close their eyes and put their heads down.

- The student at the flannel board then removes one object from the flannel board.

- On the cue "Heads up," the students try to guess which object was removed.

- The student who names the missing object first is the next one at the flannel board.

- Play several rounds. Increase the number of objects on the flannel board as students become ready for a more challenging game.

Variation
Mix the objects instead of removing one. Have the students identify the changes and rearrange the objects in their original positions.

Mother Hen and Chicks

Materials

Procedure

- Choose a student to be Mother Hen.

- The mother hen moves to the front of the room and faces away from the class.

- Direct the students in the class to place their heads on their desks and cover their mouths with their crossed arms.

- Move around the classroom and tap three students on the shoulder. These students will be the chicks.

- Give a cue such as "all ready" to the mother hen.

- On the cue, the mother hen turns around to face the class and says "Cluck cluck" to the chicks.

- The three students reply "Peep peep." All other students remain quiet.

- The mother hen listens to the reply of the chicks and taps three students who could be the chicks. If the mother hen correctly names all three chicks, that student plays another round.

- If the mother hen is incorrect, choose another student and continue the game.

Seasonal Variations

Halloween black cat (meow) and her kittens (mew), Santa Claus (ho ho) and elves (hee hee)

Five-Minute Barnyard Bingo

Materials
paper, pencil

Procedure

- Direct students to choose any five numbers from one to fifteen and write them on a piece of paper.

- Tell each student to think of any barnyard animal.

- Explain that you will call out numbers from one to fifteen. Students are to make their barnyard animal's sound and cross off the correct number on their paper each time one of their numbers is called.

- When all five numbers on a student's paper are crossed off, the student should stand.

- The first student to stand is the winner.

Pencil-Cross Observation Game

Materials
two pencils

Procedure

- Instruct the players to arrange their chairs in a circle.

- Explain to the students that they will pass the pencils around the circle. They may cross the pencils or not, but for each student there is a correct way.

- After each pass, say "Correct" or "Incorrect" to clue the students about the pattern for passing the pencils. Students should try to guess the pattern.

  Note: The passing is correct depending on the position of a student's feet. If a player's feet are crossed, then the pencils should be crossed. If the feet are uncrossed, the pencils should be uncrossed as they are passed.

Graph Paper Drawing

Materials
½″ or ¼″ graph paper

pencil

Procedure
Distribute the paper and read
the following directions:

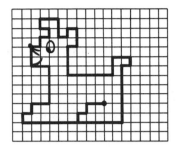

- Turn your paper horizontally.

- Find the right end of the
  horizontal line that is closest to
  the bottom edge of the paper.

- Count seven full spaces to the left.

- Move up four full spaces.

- Make a dot on the intersection of the horizontal and
  vertical lines.

- Keep your pencil on the paper and move your pencil:

left 2 spaces	up 3 spaces	left 1 space
down 1 space	right 1 space	down 1 space
left 1 space	up 2 spaces	left 1 space
down 1 space	left 1 space	down 2 spaces
right 5 spaces	down 1 space	right 2 spaces
up 6 spaces	left 1 space	down 4 spaces
right 1 space	up 2 spaces	left 2 spaces
up 1 space	left 2 spaces	down 1 space
left 2 spaces	down 1 space	left 1 space
down 2 spaces	right 1 space	down 1 space
left 5 spaces	down 1 space	right 6 spaces

- Add an eye, a mouth, a nose, and whiskers to your drawing.

  Note: For more activities like this one, try the books *Grid
  and Bear It* and *Grid and Graph It*. See the Resource Guide
  for details.

Memory

Materials

Twelve to fifteen items that are ordinarily found in a classroom, for example: eraser, pencil, ruler, chalk, book, and so on.

paper, pencil

Procedure

- Show the class the total collection of objects, one object at a time.

- Direct the students to close their eyes. Remove the objects from view.

- Tell the students to open their eyes and write as many of the objects as they can remember on their papers.

Hot Potato

Materials

several bean bags

Procedure

- Direct the students to sit in a circle.

- Choose one of the students to be the clapper. The clapper stands outside the circle and faces away from the class.

- Give bean bags to several of the students in the circle. The bean bags are the hot potatoes.

- The students begin tossing the bags from one to another until the clapper claps.

- When the clapper claps, the students who are caught holding the potatoes move to the center of the circle.

- Remove extra bean bags as the number of students in the circle decreases.

- The student who is the last one in the game is the winner. The winner becomes the next clapper.

Dog and Bone

Materials
chalkboard eraser or ruler

Procedure
- Choose a student to be the dog.
- Have the dog sit in a chair at the front of the classroom. The dog should face away from the class.
- Place the chalkboard eraser or ruler (the bone) on the floor behind the dog.
- Tap a student from the class. This student is to steal the bone quietly from behind the dog.
- The dog barks if he or she hears the bone being stolen.
- The student who can successfully steal the bone without being detected becomes the new dog.

Variations
Seasonal adaptations include: Witch and Broom, Farmer and Turkey, Santa and Toy.

Upset the Fruit Basket

Materials
none

Procedure
- Assign each student the name of a fruit. Give several students the same fruit name.
- Call out the name of one or two fruits. All students who are assigned those fruit names should switch seats.
- After a few rounds, say "Upset the fruit basket!" When this is said, all students must change seats.
- Add variety. Remove one seat and choose one student to be the fruit caller. On the cue to upset the fruit basket, the student caller hurries to get a seat, and the student who is left without a seat becomes the next caller.

Button, Button

Materials
small button or coin

Procedure

- Arrange the students in a circle.

- Direct the students to sit with their hands cupped behind them.

- Choose one student to be the first passer. Give the button to that student.

- Choose a second student to be the first guesser. The guesser stands in the center of the circle.

- Have the passer walk around the circle and pretend to put the button in every hand. The passer places the button in one student's hands, continues around the circle, and finds a seat.

- The guesser has three chances to name the person who is holding the button. If the guesser correctly identifies the student who is holding the button, he or she becomes the next passer. If the guesses are incorrect, the student who is holding the button becomes the next passer.

Who Is Knocking at My Door?

Materials
hardcover book

Procedure

- Choose a student to be the listener. The listener sits in the front of the classroom and faces away from the class.

- Have another student, the visitor, walk up behind the listener. The visitor carries the hardcover book, moves close to the listener, and knocks twice on the book.

- The listener asks, "Who is knocking at my door?"

- The visitor replies, "It is I."

- The listener may make three guesses to identify the visitor's name after hearing the voice.

- If the guess is correct, the listener plays another round. If the listener does not identify the visitor, the visitor becomes the next listener.

Variation
The visitors may knock and reply "It is I" from their seats. Direct students to switch seats quietly so the listener cannot recognize the visitor by location.

Seven Up

Materials
none

Procedure

- Select seven students (or fewer if the class size is less than twenty-one).

- Direct the remaining students to put their heads down on their desks, close their eyes, and stick up their thumbs.

- When the students are ready, silently indicate to the seven who are standing to move quietly around the room. Each of these seven students is to touch the thumb of one classmate and then return quietly to the front of the room.

- When all seven students have returned to the front of the room, say "Heads up, seven up!"

- The seven students whose thumbs were tapped should stand up. Each student may make one guess to identify the person who made the tap. If the student guesses correctly, he or she exchanges places with the tapper. If the guess is incorrect, the tapper remains up front.

- After the seven students have made their guesses, say "Heads down" and indicate to the seven tappers that they may tap different students for the next round.

Detective

Materials
none

Procedure

- Choose one student to be the detective. Have the detective walk up to the front of the classroom and face the chalkboard.

- Have the rest of the class stand in a circle. Silently point to (choose) a student leader. The class should know who the leader is, but the detective should not.

- On a cue such as "All ready," the detective turns around. The student leader carefully makes a motion, and the rest of the class makes the same motion.

- The leader tries to change the motions when the detective is not looking.

- The detective tries to discover which student is the leader. After a period of time, the detective takes three guesses. If the detective guesses correctly, he or she chooses the next detective.

- If the detective doesn't identify the leader, then the leader becomes the next detective.

- Choose another leader.

Stand Clap Relay

Materials
none

Procedure

- Divide the class into teams by rows.

- On a cue such as "Go," the first students in each row stand to the right of their seats, clap their hands twice, and sit down.

- The next students repeat these actions, and the relay continues until the students have stood, clapped, and sat down.

- When the last student in each row is seated, he or she taps the player ahead. The tapped player stands again, claps twice, sits down, and then taps the player ahead.

- Each student repeats these actions in sequence. The first team to complete the relay is the winner.

Pop-Up-and-Duck-Down Relay

Materials
none

Procedure

- Divide the class into teams by rows.

- Direct all the students to put their heads down on their folded arms.

- On a cue such as "Go," the last student in each row pops up and taps the next student in the seat in front. Then the student who was tapped pops up and taps the next student. This chain of taps continues until the first student in the row receives a tap.

- When the first person in the row is tapped, he or she pops up, turns around, whispers "Duck" to the person behind, and then sits down in the starting position (head down on folded arms).

- Again the chain is continued until the last person in the row is seated in the starting position. The first row to have completed the relay with all members down and in the starting position is the winner.

Overhead Ruler-Pass Relay

Materials
one ruler for each team

Procedure

- Divide the class into teams by rows.
- Give the first student on each team a ruler.
- Instruct the students to hold the ruler with both hands, one hand at each end of the ruler.
- The second student uses both hands and takes hold of the ruler in the center. Then the student adjusts the hold on the ruler so that both hands are at opposite ends of the ruler. The ruler is passed in this manner to the third student.
- The relay continues until the last student in the row receives the ruler. The ruler pass is then reversed and the ruler is passed in the same manner from the back of the row to the front.
- When the first students receive the ruler, they stand and hold the ruler overhead. The team whose first player stands first is the winner.

Silent Ball

Materials
small rubber ball or Nerf Ball

Procedure

- Direct the students to sit on their desktops. No feet may touch the floor.
- The students must pass the ball from one to another without talking or dropping the ball.
- Any student who talks, drops the ball, or makes a careless pass that causes the receiving student to drop the ball is out and must be seated on a chair.
- The game continues until one student remains. That student is the winner.

Wastebasket Ball

Materials
three chalkboard erasers
or three bean bags

wastebasket

chalk or tape

Procedure

- Divide the class into two teams.

- Place the wastebasket in front of the classroom and make a boundary line with chalk or a piece of tape. The line should be eight to ten feet from the wastebasket.

- Have the two teams line up behind the boundary line and face the wastebasket.

- Each player must step up to the boundary line and throw the erasers or bean bags into the wastebasket.

- Alternate between teams.

- Score a point for each eraser or bean bag that lands in the wastebasket.

- The team that scores the higher number of points is the winner.

OUTDOOR GAMES

These games are ideal for releasing pent-up energy, rewarding a class for good behavior, or for having great fun! Nearly all activities can be easily adjusted to suit any age group, but generally, the games that are best suited to younger students are presented first, and the more complex games follow.

Necessary materials are few and simple; most necessary items are standard equipment in schools. One activity, "Steal the Bacon," calls for an Indian club which may be difficult to find. For this game, simply substitute a bean bag or other easy-to-grasp object. Suggestions for relays can be found at the end of the section.

For further suggestions of outdoor games, read *Outrageous Outdoor Games*. See the Resource Guide for details.

Duck, Duck, Goose

Materials

Procedure

- Direct the students to sit in a circle on the floor and cross their legs.

- Choose one student as the tapper. The tapper walks around the circle and taps each player on the head. With each tap the tapper says "Duck," until tapping one of the students and saying "Goose."

- The student who has been tapped as the goose jumps up and chases the tapper around the circle. The goose tries to tag the tapper.

- If the tapper is tagged before reaching the space vacated by the goose, he or she must sit in the center of the circle until another tapper is caught.

- If the tapper is not tagged, he or she may play one more round as the tapper. Allow a maximum of two rounds for any student to be the tapper, and then choose a new tapper.

Back-to-Back

Materials

Procedure

- Have each student choose a partner and stand back-to-back with the partner.

- Choose one student to be the first loner.

- The loner calls out "Change," and everyone runs to find a new partner. The loner tries to get a partner also. The student who is left without a partner becomes the next loner.

The Squirrel and the Nut

Materials
a nut, such as an acorn, a buckeye, or a walnut

(If a nut is not available, a small ball or a coin will suffice.)

Procedure
- Direct the students to stand in a circle. Have them cup their hands and hold them behind their backs.
- Choose one student to be the first squirrel. The squirrel has the nut and walks around the outside of the circle.
- At one point the squirrel places the nut in the hands of one of the players.
- The player who receives the nut must chase the squirrel around the circle. The squirrel must try to reach the vacant place before being tagged.
- If the squirrel is tagged, the chaser becomes the next squirrel. If the squirrel successfully reaches the vacant place in the circle, he or she may take the nut and play the squirrel for another round.

Charlie over the Water

Materials
none

Procedure
- Direct the students to stand in a circle and join their hands.
- Choose a student to be "Charlie." Have Charlie stand in the center of the circle.
- The circle moves clockwise and the students chant:
  > Charlie over the water,
  > Charlie over the sea,
  > Charlie can catch a blackbird,
  > But can't catch me.
- On the word *me*, all students squat down quickly. Charlie attempts to tag any student before he or she squats down.
- The tagged student becomes the next Charlie.

Animal Chase

Materials
none

Procedure
- Divide the students into three or four teams.
- Assign each team an animal name.
- Designate one area on each end of the playing space as "corrals." Direct all the students to stand in one of the corrals.
- Select one student to be the first trainer.
- The trainer calls an animal name. All the students who are on the team that has that animal name must run to the other corral.
- The trainer tries to tag one of the running students.
- The tagged student becomes the next trainer.
- Play several rounds.

Two Deep

Materials
none

Procedure
- Direct the students to stand in a circle and face the center.
- Choose one student to be the chaser and one student to be the runner. The runner and chaser stand outside the circle.
- On a signal, the chaser tries to tag the runner. The runner runs in either direction around the circle. When the chaser tags the runner, the positions change immediately, and the runner becomes the chaser. The game continues in this manner.
- Either runner can move to safety by stepping in front of any player in the circle. When this happens that player in the circle becomes a runner.
- After a period of time, change the runners and chasers so that many students have a chance to run.

Octopus

Materials
none

Procedure

- Choose a student to be the octopus. Direct the octopus to stand in the center of the playing area.

- Direct the remaining students to stand at one end of the playing area. When the octopus calls "Fishies, fishies, swim around," the students must run from one end of the playing area to the other.

- The octopus tries to tag as many students as possible.

- The students that are tagged must freeze and hold their arms out from their sides.

- Again the octopus calls for the fish to swim and the remaining students must run from their places at the end of the playing area to the other end.

- This time all the students who were caught become tentacles and may tag any running player. However, only the octopus and the untagged students may move their feet.

- Play continues until only one player remains untagged. That player becomes the next octopus.

Midnight

Materials
none

Procedure

- Designate one end of the play area as the den and the other end as the safety zone.

- Choose one student to be the fox. The fox stands in the den.

- The remaining students are chickens. The chickens stand between the safety zone and the den.

- The chickens approach the fox steadily. As they move closer, they ask, "What time is it?"

- Each time the question is asked, the fox replies with any clock time or other time-related answers such as *dinnertime, very late, bedtime,* and so on. Each time the fox answers, the chickens must move closer and ask the time again.

- At some point the fox answers "Midnight!" On this cue the chickens turn and run to the safety zone. The fox chases the chickens.

- Chickens that are caught must return to the den with the fox. They help the fox chase the remaining chickens until one student is left.

- The last student to be tagged is the winner and becomes the next fox.

Cat and Mouse

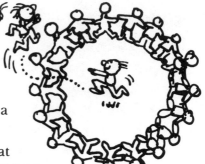

Materials
none

Procedure

- Direct the students to stand in a circle and hold hands.

- Choose one student to be the cat and another student to be the mouse.

- The mouse stands inside the circle and the cat stands outside. The students in the circle move clockwise.

- When you clap your hands, the circle must stop moving, and the cat darts inside to chase the mouse. The mouse may run outside the circle. As the cat tries to tag the mouse, the students on the circle help the mouse by raising and lowering their arms so the mouse can dart in and out. They also use their arms to barricade the cat.

- Set a time limit so that several students have the opportunity to be the cat or the mouse.

Run for Your Supper

Materials
none

Procedure

- Direct the students to stand in a circle and hold hands.

- Choose one player to be the ax. The ax walks around the circle.

- Using one hand, the ax must try to break the grasped hands of two students. When a grasp is broken, the ax calls, "Run for your supper!"

- The two students whose grasps were broken run around the circle in opposite directions. The ax takes one of their places in the circle.

- The first student to arrive back in place and grab the hand of the ax is the winner. The winner becomes the next ax. The second player to arrive returns to the circle for the next round.

Numbers Change

Materials
none

Procedure

- Number the students from one to the number of students in the class. Choose one student to be the caller.

- Direct the students to stand in a circle. Have the caller stand in the center. Students in the circle should not be in numerical order.

- The caller calls two numbers. The players whose numbers were called must run to switch places. The caller attempts to take one of the emptied spaces.

- The player who is left without a place becomes the next caller, and the game continues.

Circle Stride Ball

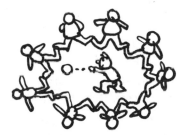

Materials
one playground ball

Procedure

- Direct the students to stand in a circle in a stride position— their feet touching the feet of the players standing on both sides.

- Choose a player to stand in the center with the ball. This player tries to roll the ball through the legs of any player in the circle.

- Circle players may use their hands to stop the ball, but they may not move their feet.

- When the center player successfully rolls the ball through a circle player's legs, that circle player takes the position of the center player and the center player joins the circle.

Streets and Alleys

STREETS

ALLEYS

Materials
none

Procedure

- Organize the students in four or five equal rows about three feet apart. Have the students join hands with the students on both sides of them. This formation is called *streets*.

- Direct the students to drop their hands and turn so that they face to their rights. Have them join hands with the players on both sides again. Adjust their spacing to three feet. This formation is called *alleys*.

- Have the students practice switching from streets to alleys. Call the two positions a few times. Students must drop their hands, turn in the correct direction, and rejoin hands. When all the students respond correctly to the calls *streets* and *alleys*, begin the game.

- Choose two students—one to be the cop and the other to be the robber. The cop chases the robber up and down the streets and alleys.

- Give a signal to start the chase, then make the game more interesting by frequently calling, "Streets" and "Alleys." The players switch their positions and the cop and robber must adjust their chase accordingly.

- Once the robber is tagged, or after a given period of time, choose other students to be the cop and the robber.

Steal the Bacon

Materials
one Indian club

Procedure

- Divide the class into two teams.

- Direct the teams to stand in parallel lines facing each other. The lines should be about fifteen to twenty feet apart.

- Place the Indian club in the center of the playing area.

- Have the students on each team count off. The teams count from opposite ends so that each player numbered *one* will be facing the last student on the opposite team. All students must remember their numbers.

- Call a number. The two players who have that number must run to snatch the Indian club.

- The player who grabs the club first must return to the starting place without being tagged. If successful, a point is scored for the team.

- The player who doesn't snatch the club can steal the point if he or she tags the player with the club before that player reaches the starting space.

- If the club is grasped at the same time by both players, it is a draw and no point is scored.

Call Ball

Materials
a large rubber playground ball

Procedure

- Direct the students to stand in a circle. Choose one student to be the caller. The caller stands in the center of the circle and holds the ball.

- The caller tosses the ball into the air and calls one student's name. That student must try to catch the ball before it bounces more than once. If successful, the catcher becomes the next caller.

- If the catcher does not get the ball before the second bounce, the caller may have another turn at calling a student's name and playing another round.

Monkey in the Middle

Materials
one rubber playground ball

Procedure

- Direct the students to stand in a circle. Choose one player to be the monkey. The monkey stands in the center of the circle.

- The players in the circle must pass the ball back and forth across the circle to one another. The student in the center tries to intercept the ball.

- If the monkey intercepts the ball, the student who threw the intercepted pass becomes the next monkey.

Running Round

Materials
one rubber playground ball

Procedure
- Direct the students to stand in a tight circle. Have one student hold the ball.

- Choose one player to be the tagger. The tagger stands outside the circle.

- The players on the circle pass or toss the ball to one another. The tagger tries to tag any player who is holding the ball.

- When the tagger successfully tags a player with the ball, that player becomes the next tagger. If a player drops the ball, he or she exchanges places with the tagger.

Dodgeball

Materials
one rubber playground ball

Procedure
- Direct the students to count off with ones and twos. Have the ones stand in a circle and the twos stand in the center of the circle.

- The players forming the circle must toss the ball and try to hit the players in the center. All hits must be made below the waist.

- Players in the center move, jump, and dodge to try to avoid being hit.

- When a center player is hit, he or she must join the circle.

- The last student inside the circle is the winner. Play a second round, and switch the center players with the circle players of the first round.

Variation
Roll Dodgeball
Play is the same except that circle players must roll the ball at the center players rather than throwing it at them.

Train Dodgeball

Materials
one rubber playground ball

Procedure

- Direct the students to stand in a circle. Choose four students to move to the center of the circle.

- The students in the center form a train by linking their arms around each other's waists. The student in the front is the engine, and the student at the end is the caboose.

- The players in the circle try to toss the ball and hit the caboose. All hits must be made below the waist.

- The engine tries to protect the caboose by batting or kicking the ball and by maneuvering the train into different locations.

- If the caboose is hit, the circle player that tossed the ball becomes the next engine. The caboose drops off the train and joins the circle. A new round of play begins.

Beat Ball

Materials
softball or similar ball

four base markers

Procedure

- Divide the class into two teams.

- Position the players on one team as if for baseball.

- Direct the players on the other team to form a line behind home base.

- Instead of batting the ball, the player at the plate throws the ball into the field. The player then runs the bases.

- The fielders throw the ball directly home to the catcher. Score one point for each base that the player touches before the ball reaches the catcher.

- There are no outs. Every player on the batting team throws the ball into the field and tries to beat the ball home.

- A ball thrown foul or caught on the fly does not score a point.

- After every player has had a turn at the plate, the teams switch positions. After both teams have had a round at the plate, the team having the higher score is the winner.

Kickball

Materials
one rubber playground ball, four base markers

Procedure
- Divide the class into two teams. Arrange one team on the field as in baseball. Extra players may stand in the outfield.

- The student pitcher rolls the ball toward the first batter of the opposite team. The kicker tries to kick the ball into the outfield.

- If the ball is fair, the kicker runs the bases.

- Follow the rules for baseball with the following exceptions:
  The kicker is out when he or she:
  is running the bases and is hit below the waist by the ball.
  kicks four foul balls.
  runs more than three feet outside the baseline to avoid being hit or tagged.

RELAY RACES

A relay race is a good way for students to release pent-up energy in a short span of time. Relays are easy to plan and often require few materials. Here are some hints about relays:

- Keep teams small, usually between four and eight players, so students don't lose interest.

- If the teams are uneven, appoint some students to run twice.

- Give clear, definite directions on how to perform the relay. Clearly designate the starting and finishing points.

- Emphasize effort. While winning is important, only a few are winners, and everyone competes.

- Adjust the length of the relay space to suit the age and ability of the grade level.

  Here is a list of ways that students can move as they compete in relays:

Early Primary

- Running
- Hopping
- Galloping
- Skipping
- Walking backward

Primary and Intermediate

- Ankle grab: Bend the knees and grab the ankles. Move forward while holding the ankles.

- Back-to-back: Stand back-to-back and link arms with a partner. Move forward to a given place in one direction. Have the partner lead on the way back.

- Ball balance: Balance a small ball on the flattened palm of one hand and move forward.

- Bear walk: Bend knees slightly. Lean over and place both hands on the ground. Move forward in this position.

- Couple dribble: Without using the hands, pass a ball back and forth to a partner and move from start to finish.

- Crab walk: From a squatting position, lean back and place both hands on the ground. Support the body weight on all four limbs in this position and move forward.

- Crossed legs: Cross one foot in front of the other. Hop forward to the finish line.

- Elephant walk: Bend forward and clasp the hands to form a "trunk." Bend and walk while swinging both arms back and forth.

- Kangaroo hop: Hold a playground ball between the knees and place both hands on the hips. Hop forward without dropping the ball.

- Lame foot: With one hand, hold one foot behind the back. Hop forward in this position.

SONGS

Singing is very helpful in the primary grades. The children enjoy singing, and they learn and use new words. The lyrics to several songs are included here. There's also a list of other songs that students are likely to know.

Use the songs as quick breaks from the routine, or sing them to reinforce listening and participation. You might want to write the words on the chalkboard if some students are unfamiliar with a song. Another way to teach the words is to speak them slowly and have the students learn them by rote. Then add the tune.

Are You Sleeping?

Are you sleeping, are you sleeping,
Brother John, Brother John?
Morning bells are ringing, morning bells are ringing,
Ding, ding, dong. Ding, ding, dong.

Eency Weency Spider

Eency weency spider went up the water spout;
Down came the rain and washed the spider out.
Out came the sun and dried up all the rain,
And the eency weency spider went up the spout again.

I'm a Little Teapot

I'm a little teapot, short and stout.
Here is my handle. Here is my spout.
When I get all steamed up, then I shout:
Tip me over and pour me out.

This Old Man

This old man, he played one.
He played nick-nack on my drum.
With a nick-nack, paddy-wack,
Give a dog a bone,
This old man came rolling home.

This old man, he played two.
He played nick-nack on my shoe.
With a nick-nack, paddy-wack,
Give a dog a bone,
This old man came rolling home.

Other verses:

three . . . knee	seven . . . oven
four . . . floor	eight . . . gate
five . . . hive	nine . . . spine
six . . . sticks	ten . . . hen

I've Been Workin' on the Railroad

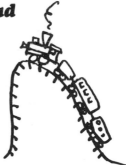

I've been workin' on the railroad,
All the live-long day;
I've been workin' on the railroad,
Just to pass the time away.

Don't you hear the whistle blowin'?
Rise up so early in the morn.
Don't you hear the captain shoutin',
Dinah, blow your horn.

Dinah, won't you blow; Dinah won't you blow,
Dinah, won't you blow your horn?
Dinah, won't you blow; Dinah, won't you blow,
Dinah, won't you blow your horn?

Someone's in the kitchen with Dinah,
Someone's in the kitchen, I know.
Someone's in the kitchen with Dinah,
Strummin' on the old banjo.

Fee, fi, fiddle-ee-i-o, Fee, fi fiddle-ee-i-o,
Fee, fi, fiddle-ee-i-o, strummin' on the old banjo.

She'll Be Coming 'Round the Mountain

She'll be coming 'round the mountain,
When she comes, a-when she comes.
She'll be coming 'round the mountain when she comes.

She'll be coming 'round the mountain,
She'll be coming 'round the mountain,
She'll be coming 'round the mountain when she comes.

Other verses:
She'll be driving six white horses when she comes.

Oh, we'll all go out to meet her when she comes.

Oh, we'll all have chicken 'n' dumplings when she comes.

Clementine

In a cavern, in a canyon, excavating for a mine,
Lived a miner, forty-niner, and his daughter Clementine.

Chorus
Oh, my darlin', oh, my darlin', oh, my darlin'
      Clementine!
You are lost and gone forever, dreadful sorry, Clementine.

Light she was and like a fairy, and her shoes were number
      nine.
Herring boxes without topses, sandals were for
      Clementine.

Repeat chorus

Other Songs:

America the Beautiful

Bicycle Built for Two

Bingo

Farmer in the Dell

Head, Shoulders, Knees, and Toes

Hokey Pokey

If You're Happy and You Know It

Kookaburra

Let's Go Fly a Kite

Little Caboose Behind the Train

London Bridge

Make New Friends

Old Smokey

The People on the Bus

Ring Around the Rosie

Row, Row, Row Your Boat

Shoo Fly

Six Little Ducks

Skip to My Lou

Ten in Bed

Where is Thumbkin?

Zippity Do Da

Seasonal Songs:

Five Little Pumpkins

Frosty the Snowman

Here Comes Peter Cottontail

Jingle Bells

Over the River

RESOURCE GUIDE

These books, also from Fearon Teacher Aids, have been selected because they are easy to use, provide solid classroom-tested activities, and require minimum preparation. In addition to *Take Me Along*, any one of these resources will enhance classroom time and support classroom teachers and substitutes alike.

Creative Chalkboard Activities

by Les Landin and Frank Thibault, 32 pages, grades 1-6

This handy book has thirty-two delightful games and activities to stimulate creative thinking—brainstorming, categorizing, predicting outcomes, and drawing conclusions.

Fall Days Holiday Lingo

by Stella V. Alexandre, 80 pages, grades 3-6

Two complete games—one for Halloween, one for Thanksgiving—are easy to use in the classroom. Bingo-type games help teach holiday words, and worksheets reinforce many basic skills.

Games Make Spelling Fun

by John F. Dean, 32 pages, grades 4-8

Quick, easy games in this book supplement the spelling curriculum. Over forty different games require minimum planning and few materials.

Grid and Bear It

by Will C. Howell, 48 pages, grades 1-3

The thirty-two reproducible activities in this book combine art and math, improve listening skills, and develop readiness for coordinate graphing. Completely reproducible materials, including graph paper, make preparation simple.

Grid and Graph It

by Will C. Howell, 48 pages, grades 4–6

Like *Grid and Bear It,* this book presents activities that are easy to plan and prepare. Versatile activities can be used to reinforce listening skills or develop graphing abilities. All grid sheets are included and are reproducible.

Help! for Primary Art

by Belva Lightner Hough, 64 pages, K–3

Twenty-four no-mess, no-fail lessons are fully illustrated with step-by-step instructions. Minimum preparation is required.

Incredible Indoor Games

by Bob Gregson, 192 pages, grades K–12

A combination of new games and traditional favorites makes these 160 projects, games, and activities a valuable collection for rainy-day, any-day fun.

Lifesavers for Teachers

by Marilyn Burch, 64 pages, grades K–3

Gamelike and cut-and-paste activities in this book require little preparation and few materials. Students enjoy these activities in reading, math, language arts, creative writing, and art. Award certificates are useful in any classroom.

Math Cut-Ups

by Ginger Wentrcek, 48 pages, grades 1–3

For basic math skills practice, these cut-and-paste worksheets take the drudgery out of drill.

Outrageous Outdoor Games

by Bob Gregson, 192 pages, grades K–12

For fill-in time, or all-day play, these exciting games give students a chance to let off steam and develop creativity in outdoor play. Preparation time is minimal; materials are readily available.

Paper Stories

by Jean Stangl, 96 pages, grades 1–3

This is a captivating collection of original stories and poems for youngsters. Tell each story with paper cutouts. All reproducible patterns make preparation easy and story time fun.

Quick 'n' Easy Learning Tasks

by Charlene Lutz, 128 pages, grades 1–4

More than ninety worksheets put students on target for learning. For each of nine subject areas there are work-sheets, a poster, and a reward certificate—all reproducible.

Reaching for Language Creativity

by Rosemary E. Runjamin, 64 pages, grades 4–6

This resource has original lessons for creative writing that engage students in brainstorming, planning, analyzing, and proposing plans. Each lesson is contained in one repro-ducible page for easy preparation.

Reading Around Town

by Elaine Prizzi and Jeanne Hoffman, 48 pages, grades 4–6

Reproducible worksheets and detailed lesson plans make this a source of functional reading fun. Students read maps, timetables, state park information, and more.

Reading Around the World

by Elaine Prizzi and Jeanne Hoffman, 48 pages, grades 4–6

These useful lessons are great as supplements to any reading lesson. Students read menus, forms, and catalogs.

Reading Everyday Stuff

by Elaine Prizzi and Jeanne Hoffman, 48 pages, grades 4–6

Students read instructions, labels, recipes, safety informa-tion, advertisements, and more. Instant activities with detailed lesson plans make this resource a perfect supple-ment anytime.

Shape-a-Poem

by Janice Auld, 48 pages, grades 1-3

Each of the fourteen lessons focuses on a poetic device or form and includes vocabulary suggestions and ideas for extensions. Reproducible shaped writing paper and booklet covers spark students' imaginations.

Shape-a-Sound

by Marilyn Burch, 48 pages, grades 1-3

Stretch creative thinking and provide practice in phonics and creative writing. Each of forty-four activities has a story starter, a reproducible writing shape, and a vocabulary list.

Shape-a-Story

by Janice Auld, 48 pages, grades 1-3

Give creative writing a new twist with these easy-to-use lessons. Story starter ideas, vocabulary lists, and reproducible writing paper shapes and booklet covers are provided.

Teachers' Holiday Helpers

by Judy Beach and Kathleen Spencer, 32 pages, grades K-3

Halloween, Thanksgiving, Christmas, Valentine's Day, Springtime

For each of the five books, there are twenty activity sheets plus a calendar, an original poem, and a finger-puppet page. Students in the primary grades practice basic skills in reading, math, language, and art. All activities are reproducible for easy preparation.

Think! Draw! Write! Level One, grades 1-3
Think! Draw! Write! Level Two, grades 4-6

by Jean Marzollo and Katherine Martin Widmer, 48 pages each

Exciting reproducible activities inspire students to conceptualize, draw, and write about ideas. Topics include parents, foods, pets, dreams, and books.

Winter Days Holiday Lingo

> by Stella V. Alexandre, 80 pages, grades 1–3
>
> Two complete games—one for Valentine's Day, one for Presidents' Day—are easy to use in the classroom. Research worksheets and art projects make these bingo-type games instructional.

Writing Well

> by John F. Dean, 64 pages, grades 5–7
>
> Students practice writing interviews, notes and letters, descriptions, and travelogs. Lesson plans that outline topics, vocabulary, and presentation techniques minimize preparation time.